D1607052

Jumpstarters
for
Science Vocabulary

Short Daily Warm-ups for the Classroom

By
LINDA ARMSTRONG

COPYRIGHT © 2009 Mark Twain Media, Inc.

ISBN 978-1-58037-489-7

Printing No. CD-404108

Mark Twain Media, Inc., Publishers
Distributed by Carson-Dellosa Publishing Company, Inc.

Visit us at www.carsondellosa.com

Table of Contents

Introduction to the Teacher

It is important for students to review information they have previously learned. *Jumpstarters for Science Vocabulary* helps them do just that, while preparing them for the day's lesson by focusing on the topic of study.

The short warm-ups in this book include matching, fill-in, and other activities to help students build and maintain a powerful science vocabulary. Each page contains five warm-ups (one for each day of the school week).

Suggestions for using *Jumpstarters* warm-up activities include:

- Copy and cut apart one page each week. Give students one warm-up activity each day at the beginning of class.
- Give each student a copy of the entire page to keep in their binders and complete as assigned.
- Make transparencies of individual warm-ups and complete or correct the activities as a group.
- Put copies of warm-ups in a learning center for students to complete on their own.
- Use as homework assignments.
- Use warm-ups as questions for a review game such as a science bee.
- Use warm-ups as a quick activity before dismissal.

Ideas for reviewing and expanding science vocabulary include:

- Play hangman using science words.
- Generate crossword puzzles online for centers, homework, or extra credit.
- Generate word searches with clues online.
- Host frequent class discussions of science topics using correct terminology.
- Encourage students to use accurate scientific vocabulary to state and defend their explanations and observations.
- Encourage students to read about science. Excellent up-to-date materials are available from the library or online.
- Review Greek and Latin word roots.
- Emphasize the importance of precise terminology when writing about topics in mathematics and science.

Science Vocabulary Warm-ups: General Science

Name/Date _____

General Science 1

Fill in the missing letters.

1. small piece   p __ r __ __ c __ __
2. way of working   me __ __ o __
3. knowledge   __ c __ __ __ c __
4. grow larger   __ xp __ __ __
5. get smaller   c __ __ t __ a __ __

Name/Date _____

General Science 2

Use the clues to unscramble these words.

1. an idea proven to be true:
   ctaf _____
2. a group of organized, related things:
   emysst _____
3. something that makes something else happen: **seuca** _____
4. something that has been made to happen:
   ctffee _____

Name/Date _____

General Science 3

Draw lines to match the words with their meanings.

1. concept   write down or save
2. observe   find similarities
3. compare   find differences
4. contrast   idea
5. record   watch

Name/Date _____

General Science 4

Fill in the missing letters.

1. a final decision, answer, or ending
   c __ __ c __ __ s __ __ n
2. facts, ideas, or information   __ __ t __
3. gather together   c __ __ __ e __ t
4. studying the parts of a whole
   __ n __ l __ s __ __
5. an ordered way of thinking   l __ __ i __

Name/Date _____

General Science 5

Fill in the blank with the correct word from the box.

repeat	experiment
identify	theory
hypothesis	

1. a logical, testable explanation _____
2. an explanation made as a starting place for discussion _____
3. a controlled test made to gain knowledge _____
4. to define or name something _____
5. to do or say again _____

Science Vocabulary Warm-ups: General Science

Name/Date _____

General Science 6

Circle the best meaning for each word.

1. term: word   bird   rock
2. grid: oil   time   mesh
3. simple: old   basic   belief
4. complex: complicated   easy   fast
5. compound: flat   combination   single

Name/Date _____

General Science 7

Draw lines to match words with meanings.

1. state   basic
2. force   move
3. fundamental   temporary form
4. flow   part
5. unit   energy

Name/Date _____

General Science 8

Read each clue. Unscramble the word.

1. to research: **iesntigatev** _____

2. a skilled way of working: **uechteqni** _____

3. to define size, weight, or temperature: **sureame** _____

4. a state of being, such as sickness or health: **itioncodn** _____

5. something that has mass and occupies space: **ansustceb** _____

Name/Date _____

General Science 9

Write the best word on each line.

phenomenon, supplemental, finite, infinite

1. _____ means limited.
2. _____ means without limits.
3. _____ means additional or extra.
4. A _____ is something you experience with your senses.

Name/Date _____

General Science 10

Write T for true or F for false.

____ 1. A *category* is a kind of panther.
____ 2. The word *rapid* means very fast.
____ 3. To *combine* means to take apart.
____ 4. If something is *toxic*, it is poisonous.
____ 5. To *penetrate* means to measure.

Science Vocabulary Warm-ups: General Science

Name/Date _____

_____

General Science 11

Write the word from the box that matches each clue.

| volume | mass | weight |
| density | speed | |

1. mass per measured unit of an object; compactness

   _____

2. rate of motion; fast or slow

   _____

3. amount of matter an object contains

   _____

4. amount of space an object occupies

   _____

5. heaviness or lightness of an object

   _____

Name/Date _____

General Science 12

Circle the best meaning for each word.

1. device: animal   cloud   instrument
2. occur: expand   happen   observe
3. abundant: rare   interesting plentiful
4. origin: beginning   part   chain
5. transform: expand   compare   change

Name/Date _____

General Science 13

Circle True or False for each statement.

1. When a planet *rotates*, it turns on its axis. True   False
2. A *component* is a kind of fish. True   False
3. To *alternate* means to go back and forth. True   False
4. A *cycle* is something that happens once and stops.
   True   False

Name/Date _____

General Science 14

Draw lines to match each term to its meaning.

1. kilogram   a hundredth of a meter
2. gram   basic metric unit of weight
3. milligram   a thousandth of a meter
4. millimeter   a thousandth of a gram
5. centimeter   a thousand grams

Name/Date _____

General Science 15

Unscramble each word to match the clue.

1. **eureteratmp** _____ heat or cold
2. **siCusel** _____ metric temperature scale
3. **gdreee** _____ unit of temperature measurement
4. **hreFheanit** _____ temperature scale used in the U.S.A.

Science Vocabulary Warm-ups: General Science

Name/Date _____

General Science 16

Use each clue to unscramble the word.

1. take in   **sobarb** _____
2. equality   **lceanba** _____
3. power to float **uoycyban** _____
4. a particular quality

   actticarerchsi _____
5. sort   **ssayifcl** _____

Name/Date _____

General Science 17

Draw lines connecting clues to terms.

1. width   evaluate
2. most important   evidence
3. judge results   flow chart
4. data supporting   dominant
   a conclusion
5. diagram showing   diameter
   steps

Name/Date _____

General Science 18

Fill in the missing letters.
1. assigned duty   f __ __ ct __ __ n
2. reasoning from something known
   __ n __ __ r __ __ __ e
3. inquire or examine
   in __ __ __ ti __ a __ e
4. meters and kilograms
   m __ __ __ __ c measurements
5. description used for discussion and
   investigation   m __ d __ l

Name/Date _____

General Science 19

Circle the clue that matches each word.

1. act of moving: dominance   movement
2. object: thing   phase
3. observing: noticing   flowing
4. phase: evidence   stage
5. predict: believe   foretell

Name/Date _____

General Science 20

Write the correct term from the box on each line.

property	purpose
scientific explanations	
scientific procedures	
sequence	

1. reason for existing _____
2. order _____
3. a distinctive quality _____
4. statements based on logic, observation, and testing _____
5. logical, orderly working methods _____

Science Vocabulary Warm-ups: General Science

Name/Date _____

General Science 21

thriving	transfer
variables	volume
Venn diagram	

Write the word from the box that best completes each sentence.

1. He drew a _____ to show which animals ate both insects and seeds.

2. The _____ of the tank was 38 cubic meters.

3. The meadow was a _____ community of plants and animals.

4. Temperature, rainfall, and wind direction were important _____.

5. Genes _____ information from one generation to the next.

Name/Date _____

General Science 22

Write the word that best fits each clue.

stable, structure, system, technique

1. constant, maintaining form
   _____

2. the way tissues, organs, or rock layers are arranged _____

3. way of working _____

4. a group of objects or parts acting together _____

Name/Date _____

General Science 23

Circle the word that best fits each clue.

1. order: segment   sequence   variable

2. outcome: cause   system   result

3. exact: precise   estimate   volume

4. part: segment   system   biome

5. identify: assume   decay   name

Name/Date _____

General Science 24

Circle T for true or F for false.

1. *Efficiency* means the best use of energy. T F

2. To *assume* means to prove. T F

3. To *extend* means to stretch out. T F

4. To *belong* means to be left out. T F

5. To *conclude* means to observe. T F

Name/Date _____

General Science 25

Fill in the missing letters.

1. The temperature in the special cooler remained c __ n __ __ a __ t.

2. Hardness is one c __ __ r __ __ - t __ __ __ s __ ic of minerals.

3. When a tree falls, its wood begins to d __ __ __ y.

4. The a __ __ __ __ g __ rainfall in our town is 40 inches per year.

Science Vocabulary Warm-ups: General Science

Name/Date _____

General Science 26

Write the word that best completes each sentence.

interference   **equilibrium**   **imbalance**

1. Snowfall and melting reached an _____, and the glacier stopped growing.

2. An _____ in squirrel birth and death rates caused overpopulation.

Name/Date _____

General Science 27

Use the clues to unscramble the words.

1. sensible: **bsonaealer** _____
2. measure: **afyntiqu** _____
3. become larger: **crseeina** _____
4. reaction: **nesrpose** _____

Name/Date _____

General Science 28

Write the best word in each blank.

HYPOTHESIS

valid   **series**   **test**   **study**

In a recent year-long (1) _____, scientists ran a (2) _____ of experiments to (3) _____ Professor Kramer's hypothesis. They had to be sure that his explanation was (4) _____.

Name/Date _____

General Science 29

Draw a line to connect the word with its definition.

1. collide   does not change
2. absolute   depends upon changing conditions
3. principles   run into each other
4. relative   fundamental rules or laws

Name/Date _____
_____

General Science 30

Fill in the missing letters.

1. a well-established observation about nature

   __ c __ e __ ti __ __ c

   l __ __

2. a preliminary idea about how something in nature works

   s __ __ __ n __ i __ ic

   m __ d __ l

3. a testable model based on repeatable experimental evidence

   s __ ien __ __ __ ic

   __ h __ o __ y

4. use of observation and experimentation to develop and test ideas

   s __ i __ n __ __ __ ic

   m __ __ __ od

5. information supporting or disproving a scientific idea

   __ __ __ __ __ ific

   e __ __ d __ n __ e

Science Vocabulary Warm-ups: General Science

Name/Date _____

General Science 31

Draw a line from the word to the best clue.

1. reliable   carry
2. stationary   combining
3. variation   dependable
4. transport   unmoving
5. synthesis   difference

Name/Date _____

General Science 32

Circle T for true or F for false.

1. When water changes to ice, it is a reversible process. T F
2. Scientists never evaluate the results of their experiments. T F
3. If there is more food today, the quality of the food has increased. T F
4. If there is more pollution, the quantity of pollution has increased. T F

Name/Date _____

General Science 33

Write the best term on each line.

random	regulate
reject	cyclic
dehydrate	

1. You must _____ the temperature in an incubator.
2. Instead of picking particular eggs, we chose some at _____.
3. We had to _____ and discard two eggs.
4. We used warm air to _____ apricots.
5. Rainfall, runoff, and evaporation are part of a _____ process.

Name/Date _____

General Science 34

Use the clue to unscramble each word.
1. how often something happens:

   uenfrcyeq _____

2. how things depend on each other:

   onsitterreinlahip _____

3. likely: **babperol** _____
4. move away: **drecee** _____
5. move toward: **vacenad** _____

Name/Date _____

General Science 35

Draw a line to match each word with the best clue.

1. replicate   importance
2. submerge   nonliving
3. boundary   sink
4. inorganic   copy
5. significance   limit

Science Vocabulary Warm-ups: Life Science

Name/Date _____

Life Science 1

Unscramble each word.

1. **ceyoolg** _____   Study of living things in the places they live
2. **mmncotiuy** _____   Group of living things
3. **eerhpoibs** _____   All land, sea, and air containing living things
4. **eeonnnirmtv** _____   Air, sea, or land around a living thing
5. **onaaatpdti** _____   Change that helps a living thing fit its surroundings

---

Name/Date _____

Life Science 2

Fill in the missing letters.
1. Sorting items into groups
   cl __ __ __ ifi __ __ t __ __ n
2. Things that are not alive.
   __ __ __ l __ __ __ __ g
3. Scientific term for things that are alive
   o __ g __ n __ __ __ s
4. Specific types of living things
   s __ __ c __ __ s

Name/Date _____

Life Science 3

Fill in the blanks with one of these words.
herbivores, carnivores, omnivores

1. Animals that eat only meat are
   _____.
2. Animals that eat only plants are
   _____.
3. Animals that eat meat and plants are
   _____.

Name/Date _____

Life Science 4

Circle T for true or F for false.
1. A food web includes producers, consumers, and decomposers. T F
2. A producer breaks down dead plants and animals. T F
3. A producer changes light energy to food energy. T F
4. Consumers eat producers. T F
5. A food web is a special spider web. T F

Name/Date _____

Life Science 5

Draw lines to match words to clues.

1. mammal   is an invertebrate
2. reptile   lives part of life on land
3. amphibian   and part in water
4. bird   has fur or hair
5. mollusk   has scales
                    has feathers

Science Vocabulary Warm-ups: Life Science

Name/Date _____

Life Science 6

Circle the best example for each term.

1. offspring: calf   rock   soil

2. trait: cat   ocean   eye color

3. behavior: size   diving   caves

4. habitat: chasing   howling   forest

5. juvenile: desert   kitten   markings

Name/Date _____

Life Science 7

Fill in the blank with the letter of the correct word.

**A. life cycle, B. maturity,
C. inheritance, D. lifespan**

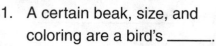

1. A certain beak, size, and coloring are a bird's _____.

2. The tadpole phase is part of a frog's ____.

3. The length of an animal's life is its _____.

4. A term for an animal's adulthood is ____.

Name/Date _____

Life Science 8

Draw lines to match terms and definitions

1. membrane   control center of a cell

2. cytoplasm   contents of a cell, except the nucleus

3. cell   tiny structures with special tasks

4. organelles   a basic unit of life

5. nucleus   a thin wall or layer

Name/Date _____

Life Science 9

Circle T for true or F for false.

1. Diversity means that only one type of animal lives an area. T F

2. Genes carry the code of heredity. T F

3. Some animals survive the winter by hibernating. T F

4. Migration is a way for animals to hide from enemies. T F

5. A larva is an adult insect. T F

Name/Date _____

Life Science 10

Circle the word that fits each meaning.

1. coloration that hides an animal: diversity   camouflage   prey

2. an animal that is hunted: transpiration   camouflage   prey

3. the act of imitating or copying: mimicry   parasitism   osmosis

4. disappearing from the earth: osmosis   extinction   transpiration

5. an animal that hunts: predator   gene   diversity

Science Vocabulary Warm-ups:
Life Science

Name/Date _____

Life Science 11

Circle the word or words in each line that are parts of a tree.

1. branch   crown
2. compost   bulb
3. cone   humus
4. needle   limb

Name/Date _____

Life Science 12

Write the letter of the best word on each line.
A. seeds, B. germinate, C. embryo, D. propagation, E. runners

Our class is studying plant (1) _____. We planted some
(2) _____. Each seed contained a baby plant, or (3) _____. It
took a week for the seeds to (4) _____. We learned that plants
do not always grow from seeds. Some grow from (5) _____.

Name/Date _____

Life Science 13

Circle the term that fits the clue.

1. creating fuel from light: photosynthesis   chlorophyll
2. location of chlorophyll: root   leaf   trunk
3. gas created through photosynthesis: oxygen   hydrogen
4. green substance in leaves: carbon dioxide   chlorophyll
5. gas used in photosynthesis: carbon dioxide   oxygen

Name/Date _____

Life Science 14

Circle T for true or F for false.

1. Soil is a combination of crumbled
   rock, humus, air, and water. T F
2. Humus is a kind of dip eaten as a snack. T   F
3. Compost can be used to enrich soils. T   F
4. Peat usually forms in swamps or bogs. T   F

Name/Date _____

_____

Life Science 15

Write the term from the box that best fits each clue.

> pistil   petal
> stigma   pollen
> ovary

1. base of the pistil, where seeds develop

   _____

2. sticky tip of the style, receives pollen

   _____

3. fertilizes ovules to create seeds

   _____

4. often colorful, helps to attract insects

   _____

5. the ovary, style, and stigma of a flower

   _____

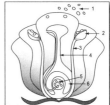

Science Vocabulary Warm-ups: Life Science

Name/Date _____

Life Science 16

Write the word that best fits each clue.

biome   physical   exchange
distribution   utility

1. trade: _____
2. usefulness: _____
3. A grassland is an example of a
   _____.
4. A rock cracking is an example of a
   _____ change.
5. spread: _____

Name/Date _____

Life Science 17

Draw a line to match each term to the best clue.

1. population   substances
2. source   group
3. convert   organization
4. structure   origin
5. materials   change

Name/Date _____

Life Science 18

Circle the term that best fits each clue.

1. related to breathing: digestion   respiration   excretion
2. related to breaking down food: digestion   respiration   excretion
3. waste disposal: digestion   respiration   excretion
4. transport of materials: digestion   circulation   regulation
5. many-celled: pituitary   temporal   multicellular

Name/Date _____

Life Science 19

Circle T for true or F for false.

1. Red blood cells are specialized to perform certain jobs. T F
2. Microorganisms live only on microscope lenses. T F
3. Pollination is often performed by insects. T F
4. Gravity, wind, and animal activities help with seed dispersal. T F

Name/Date _____

Life Science 20

Write the word that best fits each clue.

defend   descendant   survive
pest   protozoa

1. single-celled organisms: _____
2. protect: _____
3. destructive animal or plant: _____
4. offspring: _____
5. continue to live: _____

Jumpstarters for Science Vocabulary

Science Vocabulary Warm-ups: Life Science

Name/Date _____

Life Science 21

Write the letter of the best word on each line.

A. nitrogen   B. osmosis   C. niche
D. nitrogen cycle

1. _____ is the movement of a fluid through a membrane.
2. A _____ is an organism's special place in an ecosystem.
3. Most of the gas in the atmosphere is _____.
4. As part of the _____, bacteria change a gas to a form plants can use.

Name/Date _____

Life Science 22

Circle the term that best fits the clue.

1. A clear, yellowish component of blood:
   sponge   crustacean   plasma
2. A marine animal: sponge   virus   spore
3. A single cell or seed that can grow into a new organism: spore   virus   plasma
4. An animal belonging to the same family as the lobster: sponge   crustacean   virus
5. A microscopic agent that can cause disease:
   crustacean   virus   plasma

Name/Date _____

Life Science 23

Draw a line to match each term to the best clue.

1. beetle — not hatched from an egg
2. protoplasm — two species benefiting one another
3. mutualism — kind of insect
4. live birth — a species living at the expense of another
5. parasite — living matter

Name/Date _____

Life Science 24

Draw a line to match each term to the best clue.

1. gills — outside
2. mates — inside
3. internal — reaction
4. external — goose and gander
5. response — respiratory organ of a fish

Name/Date _____

Life Science 25

Use the clues to unscramble the terms.

1. Animals that produce their own body heat are: **arwm-bldeood** _____.
2. Animals with segmented bodies and outer shells such as insects: **rthroodsap** _____
3. Bacteria that live in water and produce their own food through photosynthesis: **uebl-eegrn agael** _____
4. When resources are scarce, there is: **petictionom** _____.
5. A creature's shell or hard protective layer: **esketonlxoe** _____

Life Science

Science Vocabulary Warm-ups: Human Body

Human Body 1

| abdomen |
| forearm   instep |
| thigh   calf |

Write the term from the box that best fits each clue.

1. lower leg _____
2. lower arm _____
3. arched part of foot _____
4. upper leg _____
5. belly _____

Human Body 2

Fill in the missing letters.

1. a repeated series of events c __ c __ e
2. tissues grouped together to perform a function o __ __ __ n
3. a group of similar cells acting together to perform a function t __ s __ u __
4. organs grouped together to perform a function o __ g __ __ s __ __ t __ m

---

Human Body 3

Using the clue, unscramble each word or phrase.

1. brain and spinal cord: **enalctr vusnero steysm** _____
2. center for thought and control of body functions: **nrbai** _____
3. special cells that carry information: **snveer** _____
4. cord that carries information from the brain to body: **alsinp rcod** _____
5. something that causes a response: **ultimsus** _____

Human Body 4

Write the letter of the correct term on each line.
A. circulatory system, B. heart, C. cardiac
D. chambers, E. cardiac muscle

The word (1) _____ refers to a special pump, the (2) _____. It is an important part of the (3) _____. It is made from (4) _____, and it has four sections, or (5) _____.

Human Body 5

Circle the best term or terms for each clue.

1. carries used blood back to the heart:
   artery   capillary   vein
2. carries fresh blood from the heart to the body: artery   capillary   vein
3. carries oxygen and fuel to individual cells:
   artery   capillary   vein
4. blood vessel: artery   vein   platelets
5. carries blood from the heart to the lungs:
   capillary   pulmonary artery   vein

Science Vocabulary Warm-ups: Human Body

Name/Date _____

Human Body 6

Using the clues, unscramble each term.

1. Breaks down food for use by cells in the body:

   evegtisdi _____ system

2. Pouch-like organ where food is broken down: **macohst** _____

3. Tube-like organ where food is digested and absorbed: **nestestini** _____

4. Tube from the mouth to the stomach: **ehagussop** _____

5. Releases substances that control the use of fuels from food: **vrlie** _____

Name/Date _____

Human Body 7

Fill in the missing letters.

1. Thickening of blood to stop bleeding

   co __ g __ l __ t __ __ n

2. Blood cells that carry oxygen   r __ d

3. Blood cells that defend against outside invaders   w __ __ __ e

4. Cell fragments in plasma that help clotting

   p __ __ te __ __ __ s

5. The clear liquid part of blood or lymph

   p __ __ __ m __

Name/Date _____

Human Body 8

Write the letter of the correct term on each line.

A. spine   **B. skeletal system**
C. marrow   **D. bones**

The (1) _____ supports the body. It consists of the skull, (2) _____, and the (3) _____. Tissues inside the bones, in the (4) _____ produce blood cells. This system also includes joints and connective tissue.

Name/Date _____

Human Body 9

Circle the part of the body where each can be found.

1. femur:	hips	arms	legs
2. pelvis:	hips	arms	legs
3. patella:	knee	elbow	heel
4. rib:	chest	hips	skull
5. sternum:	chest	knee	elbow

Name/Date _____

Human Body 10

Write the letter of the correct term on each line.

A. bronchial tubes, B. oxygen, C. lungs
D. respiratory system, E. diaphragm

The (1) _____ brings fresh (2) _____ into the body and carries away carbon dioxide. Powerful muscles in the (3) _____ expand the chest cavity to pull air into the (4) _____ through the (5) _____.

Science Vocabulary Warm-ups: Human Body

Name/Date _____

_____

Human Body 11

Using the clue, unscramble each boldface term.

1. Proteins, minerals, and vitamins are important **utrintsen**.

   _____

2. The food **miyrdpa** is a chart that helps people plan nutritious meals.

   _____

3. The body needs iron, calcium, and other **nalermis**.

   _____

4. A **eioalcr** is a measurement of food energy.

   _____

5. **Vnimita** C is important for good health.

   _____

Name/Date _____

Human Body 12

Circle the correct term.

1. relating to the eye: optic   auditory   dental
2. relating to hearing: optic   auditory   dental
3. part of the tooth: retina   saliva   dentin
4. fluid in the mouth: retina   saliva   dentin
5. part of the eye: retina   saliva   dentin

Name/Date _____

Human Body 13

Fill in the missing letters.

1. This type of organ produces chemicals the body needs.
   g __ __ __ d
2. This gland produces hormones. e __ __ oc __ __ n __
3. These glands release adrenaline. a __ __ e __ __ l
4. This gland produces insulin and digestive juices.
   p __ __ c __ __ __ s

Name/Date _____

Human Body 14

Draw a line to connect each clue to the correct term

1. system that moves waste out of the body   urethra
2. one of two organs that remove waste from blood   bladder
3. organ where urine is stored   excretory
4. organ that removes waste through perspiration   kidney
5. tube connecting bladder to the outside of the body skin

Name/Date _____

Human Body 15

Circle T for true or F for false.

1. The biceps is found in the leg. T   F
2. The triceps is found in the arm. T   F
3. The muscular system breaks down food for the body. T   F
4. When muscles relax, they get thicker and shorter. T   F
5. When muscles contract, they get thicker and shorter. T   F

Science Vocabulary Warm-ups: Human Body

Name/Date _____

Human Body 16

Write the letter of the best term on each line.

A. spleen   B. nodes   C. lymph
D. lymphatic system

The job of the (1) _____ is to fight infection and maintain the body's fluid balance. It carries a fluid called (2) _____ from the tissues into the bloodstream. The (3) _____ produces cells that help to fight disease. Lymph (4) _____ help to filter bacteria and waste from the lymph fluid.

Name/Date _____

Human Body 17

Place the letter of the term on the blank next to the correct definition.

____ 1. Breathing in
____ 2. Breathing out
____ 3. When the body takes in oxygen and releases carbon dioxide

A. gas exchange
B. carbon dioxide
C. inhalation
D. exhalation

____ 4. Exhaled during respiration

Name/Date _____

Human Body 18

Circle T for true or F for false.

1. Starch is found in potatoes and rice.
   T F
2. All fiber is easy to digest. T F
3. Proteins are macronutrients. T F
4. Vitamins are micronutrients. T F
5. Fats are unnecessary in a healthy diet.
   T F

Name/Date _____

Human Body 19

Unscramble each term.

1. The hard outer layer of the tooth
   eeamln _____
2. Tissue around the pulp inside the tooth
   etdinn _____
3. Part of the tooth below the gum
   orot _____
4. Part of the tooth above the gum line
   rnocw _____
5. Firm tissues around your teeth
   musg _____

Name/Date _____

Human Body 20

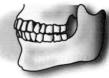

Circle the term that fits each clue.

1. Flat teeth designed for grinding	incisors	molars	deciduous
2. Sharp teeth designed for cutting	incisors	molars	deciduous
3. Teeth that fall out and are replaced	incisors	molars	deciduous
4. Teeth that do not grow back if lost	dentures	deciduous	permanent
5. Bones that hold the teeth	scapula	patella	jaw

17

Science Vocabulary Warm-ups: Human Body

Name/Date _____

Human Body 21

Unscramble each term.

1. Basic unit of heredity: **ngee** _____
2. Thread-like part of a cell that contains genes: **roommosche** _____
3. A molecule that contains coded hereditary information: **NDA** _____
4. Smallest particle of a particular compound or element: **leulecmo** _____
5. Traits passed from one generation to the next: **heyditer** _____

Name/Date _____

Human Body 22

Fill in the missing letters.
1. one-celled organisms
   b __ c __ __ r __ a
2. vaccination to create immunity
   in __ c __ l __ t __ __ n
3. a very tiny parasite or disease-causing
   agent   v __ __ __ s
4. a disease-causing agent
   p __ __ h __ g __ n

Name/Date _____

Human Body 23

Write the letter of the best term on each line.
   A. infectious   **B. immune system**
   C. lymphocytes   **D. barriers**

The (1) _____ defends the body against

(2) _____ diseases. Many (3) _____ guard

the body, including the skin.

(4) _____ in the bloodstream

attack invaders.

Name/Date _____

Human Body 24

Unscramble each term.
1. good physical condition:
   esitfns _____
2. ease of movement:
   liibifltyxe _____
3. in the presence of oxygen:
   erabico _____
4. lasting power, stamina:
   edurennca _____

Name/Date _____

Human Body 25

Place the letter of the term next to the correct definition.
   A. imaging B. prosthesis C. technology
   D. laser E. endoscope

_____ 1. applied science
_____ 2. making pictures of the inside of the body
_____ 3. device for taking pictures inside the body
_____ 4. device that replaces a body part
_____ 5. produces a very powerful beam of light

Science Vocabulary Warm-ups: Human Body

Name/Date _____

Human Body 26

Write the letter of the best term on each line.
  A. sound waves   B. vibrate   C. eardrum
  D. impulses   E. auditory canal

When (1) _____ enter the

(2) _____, they cause the

(3) _____ and tiny bones inside

the ear to (4) _____. Sensors in

the inner ear send (5) _____ to the brain.

Name/Date _____

Human Body 27

Unscramble each term.

1. sense that lets you know where you are
   in space: **bcealan** _____

2. location of balance organs:
   nnier are _____

3. three tubular canals in the inner ear:
   laemsircuicr alsnac _____

4. part of the body that receives stimuli:
   nersos _____

Name/Date _____

Human Body 28

Circle the best term to fit each clue.

1.	Light rays focus on rods and cones here.	lens	cornea	retina
2.	This flexible, clear structure controls focus in the eye.	lens	cornea	retina
3.	This is the colored part of the eye.	iris	lens	pupil
4.	This opening lets light into the eye.	iris	lens	pupil
5.	The clear outside coating of the eye.	cornea	iris	pupil

Name/Date _____

Human Body 29

Circle the four basic tastes the taste buds can detect. Write a food for each taste.

1. spicy _____
2. sweet _____
3. sour _____
4. salty _____
5. bitter _____

Name/Date _____

Human Body 30

Draw a line matching each definition to its term.

1. causes a reaction   sensitive
2. hurt   irritation
3. receptive to feeling   pain
4. soreness or inflammation   dermis
5. inner layer of skin   stimulus

Science Vocabulary Warm-ups: Earth Science

Name/Date _____

Earth Science 1

Write the best term for each clue.

outer core, mantle, crust, inner core

1. the outer layer of the earth

   _____

2. the center of the earth

   _____

3. just below the earth's outer layer

   _____

4. layer just above the earth's center

   _____

Name/Date _____

Earth Science 2

Unscramble each term.

1. recent theory that sections of the crust are in motion: plate **icsetncto** _____

2. a large land mass: **ecoinntnt** _____

3. older idea about the movement of the earth's continents: **tlcnoeatnin rdtif**

   _____

4. one of many large pieces of the earth's crust and upper mantle: **apelt** _____

Name/Date _____

Earth Science 3

Fill in the missing letters.

1. a crack in the rocky crust of the earth: f __ __ l __

2. shaking of the earth's surface caused by underground movement:

   e __ __ th __ __ a __ e

3. ripple of energy passing through rock, water, or air: w __ v __

4. machine that records ground movements:

   s __ __ s __ __ g __ __ __ h

Name/Date _____

Earth Science 4

Draw a line to match each term to the best clue.

1. seismology   size
2. shallow   shaking
3. tsunami   study of earthquakes
4. tremor   near the surface
5. magnitude   ocean wave caused

                      by an earthquake

EARTHQUAKE
EPICENTER

Name/Date _____

Earth Science 5

Write the best word from the box on each line.

interior	exterior
epicenter	occur
seismometer	

1. The part of the seismograph that measures the direction, duration, and force of an earthquake is a _____.

2. The inside of the earth is the _____.

3. The outside of the earth is the _____.

4. An earthquake's point of origin inside the earth is the _____.

5. Another word for "happen" is _____.

Science Vocabulary Warm-ups: Earth Science

Name/Date _____

Earth Science 6

Fill in the missing letters.
1. relating to a volcano: v __ __ c __ __ ic
2. powdery rock from a volcanic explosion:
   a __ __
3. hard, dark rock formed from cooled lava:
   b __ __ a __ t
4. very light-weight volcanic
   rock: p __ __ i __ e
5. glassy volcanic rock: ob __ __ d __ __ n

Name/Date _____

Earth Science 7

Write the letter for the correct term on each line.
A. crater   B. chamber   C. volcano
D. magma   E. vent

A (1) _____ is a cone-shaped mountain. It
forms when (2) _____, or molten rock, rises
from a magma (3) _____ to the surface. It
flows out through a (4) _____ at the top. After
the eruption, the top of the mountain often
caves in to form a (5) _____.

Name/Date _____

Earth Science 8

Circle the term that matches each clue.

1. poisonous: toxic   explosive   volcanic
2. able to blow up:
   solidify   explosive   volcanic
3. turn into a solid: erupt   shield   solidify
4. outpouring of lava, ash, or gases:
   eruption   shield   composite

Name/Date _____

Earth Science 9

Match each term to the correct clue.

____ 1. melted rock flowing on
         the surface
____ 2. adjective describing
         red-hot, liquid rock
____ 3. a volcano that will
         probably never erupt again
____ 4. a volcano that is not
         erupting at the moment
____ 5. a volcano that is erupting

A. active
B. dormant
C. molten
D. extinct
E. lava

Name/Date _____

Earth Science 10

Write the best word from the box on each line.

The (1) _____ _____ describes the way one kind of

rock can change into another kind of rock. For example, layers of sandstone,

a (2) _____ rock, can be melted deep inside the earth and flow out of a

volcano to become basalt, an (3) _____ rock. That basalt can be

buried under newer layers of rock. With heat and (4) _____, it can

become a (5) _____, or changed, rock called a schist.

igneous
metamorphic
pressure
sedimentary
rock cycle

Science Vocabulary Warm-ups: Earth Science

Name/Date _____

Earth Science 11

Fill in the missing letters.

1. Under heat and pressure, limestone changes to this metamorphic rock. m __ __ b __ e

2. Under heat and pressure, shale changes to this metamorphic rock. __ l __ t __

3. This igneous rock cools deep underground. g __ __ __ it __

4. rock form with a regular repeating structure: c __ __ __ t __ l

5. to change form: t __ __ __ __ f __ __ m

Name/Date _____

Earth Science 12

Draw a line to match each sedimentary rock to its source.

1. sandstone   clay

2. conglomerate   sand

3. shale   dissolved shells

4. limestone   pebbles, sand, and clay

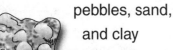

Name/Date _____

Earth Science 13

Write the best term on each line.
resistant, erosion, strata, conservation, weathering

1. layers of rock: _____

2. removal of rock by water or wind: _____

3. breaking up of rock by ice, rain, wind, or chemical action: _____

4. protecting soil from overuse or erosion: soil _____

5. able to stand up to erosion (a hard rock layer): _____

Name/Date _____

Earth Science 14

The following words are characteristics used to identify rocks and minerals. Unscramble each term.

1. lsture   _____

2. sardhnes   _____

3. olocr   _____

4. satkre rlooc   _____

5. tycrsla pehas   _____

Name/Date _____

Earth Science 15

Fill in the missing letters.

1. The most common mineral on earth: q __ __ __ __ z

2. A natural substance with a crystalline structure: m __ n __ r __ l

3. A mineral used to make pennies: c __ p __ __ r

4. A mineral known as "fool's gold": p __ r __ t __

5. A yellow mineral that smells like rotten eggs: s __ lf __ r

---

Science Vocabulary Warm-ups: Earth Science

Name/Date _____

Earth Science 16

Draw a line to match each term with an example.

1. renewable resource   wind energy
2. nonrenewable resource   smog
3. alternative energy source   forests
4. pollution   oil

Name/Date _____

Earth Science 17

Fill in the missing letters.
1. Hard coal that burns at a high temperature
   a __ t __ r __ c __ __ e
2. Soft coal that burns at lower temperatures
   b __ t __ __ i __ o __ s
3. Parts of living things turned to rock, coal, or petroleum
   fo __ __ i __ s

Name/Date _____

Earth Science 18

Write the letter of the correct word on the line.
A. topography, B. lithosphere, C. block, D. folded

____ 1. Mountains that are pushed up between two faults

____ 2. Mountains built from bent rock layers

____ 3. The top rocky layer of the crust

____ 4. The surface features of an area

Name/Date _____

Earth Science 19

Circle the correct term.

1. pushed up   compressed deposited uplifted
2. in the open   exposed compressed deposited
3. laid down   uplifted deposited compressed
4. pushed together uplifted deposited compressed

Name/Date _____

_____

Earth Science 20

Write the correct term from the box on each blank.

fossilization	skeletons
impressions	hardened
shells	

During the process of

(1) _____,

plant and animal parts are

(2) _____

into rock. Fossilized

(3) _____ of

mammals, fish, birds, and

reptiles tell us about life in the

past. (4) _____,

such as dinosaur footprints, are

fascinating fossils. Fossilized

(5) _____ of

sea creatures are very common.

Science Vocabulary Warm-ups: Earth Science

Name/Date _____

Earth Science 21

Write the letter of the correct term on the line.

**A. dunes   B. crescent   C. particles
D. deposited**

1. Sand _____ come in several shapes.
2. Sand is composed of rock _____.
3. Many dunes are _____- shaped.
4. The sand is carried and _____ by the wind.

Name/Date _____

Earth Science 22

Unscramble each term.

1. large floating chunk of ice: **ibeegrc** _____
2. melting glacier: **rtreangeti** _____
3. growing glacier: **acianndvg** _____
4. U-shaped area created by a glacier: **lyeval** _____
5. type of glacier that covers large areas of Antarctica: **cie hsete** _____

Name/Date _____

Earth Science 23

Unscramble each term.

1. Formations hanging from a cave ceiling: **iteasttlacs** _____
2. A formation on the floor of a cave: **saglitemta** _____
3. Another name for a cave: **vecran** _____
4. A substance capable of destroying or eating away: **csiorerov** _____
5. To mix with a liquid: **olsvdise** _____

Name/Date _____

Earth Science 24

Fill in the missing letters.

1. near the ocean: c __ a __ t __ l
2. curved rock formation formed by erosion: a __ __ h
3. rock column in the ocean near the shore: s __ __ __ k
4. waves wearing away the lower part of a cliff: u __ __ er __ __ t __ __ ng

---

Name/Date _____

Earth Science 25

Write the letter for the best term on each line.
**A. ground water, B. columns,
C. surface streams, D. formations, E. chambers**

Limestone caverns are often filled with beautiful (1) _____. Natural (2) _____ dissolves the rock to create underground rooms called (3) _____. Stalactites, stalagmites, and (4) _____ are like magical gardens of stone. Sometimes (5) _____ plunge down through openings to form waterfalls.

Science Vocabulary Warm-ups: Earth Science

Name/Date _____

Earth Science 26

Write the letter of the best word on each line.

**A. abyssal   B. slope   C. shelf
D. seaward   E. floor**

The ocean (1) _____ is deeper in some places than others. The continental (2) _____ lies underwater at the edge of each continent. Beyond it, in deeper water, is the continental (3) _____. On the (4) _____ side of the slope is the (5) _____ plain.

Name/Date _____

Earth Science 27

Fill in the missing letters.

1. A consistent flow of surface water is an ocean
   c __ __ __ e __ t.
2. The d __ __ t __ of the ocean varies from shallow shelves to deep trenches.
3. The saltiness of the ocean is called its
   s __ l __ __ __ t __.
4. The word m __ r __ __ e refers to the ocean.

Name/Date _____

Earth Science 28

Draw a line to match each clue to the correct term.

1. the deepest parts of the ocean floor   hot spot
2. not deep   island
3. top   trenches
4. land surrounded by water   shallow
5. place where volcanic islands form   surface

Name/Date _____

Earth Science 29

Circle the correct term.

1. middle of the ocean: sonar   mid-ocean
2. area: zone   sonar
3. used to find underwater objects: sonar   catapult
4. ocean bottom: zone   sea floor
5. landmass: sea floor   continent

Name/Date _____

Earth Science 30

Write the best word from the box on each line.

| neap | tides | bulge |
| gravity | spring | |

(1) _____ are caused by the (2) _____ of the moon pulling on the earth's oceans. The water is pulled out into a (3) _____ on either side of the planet. When the sun and moon are lined up, there are large tides called (4) _____ tides. When the sun and moon are positioned at right angles, the tides are not as high as usual. These milder changes in sea level are called (5) _____ tides.

Science Vocabulary Warm-ups: Earth Science

Name/Date _____

Earth Science 31

Underline the correct term.

1.	a river of ice:	moraine	glacier	deposit
2.	dirt and rock deposited by a glacier:	moraine	glacier	deposit
3.	period marked by the growth of glaciers:	global warming	ice age	abrasion
4.	wearing away:	deposition	glaciation	abrasion
5.	laying down:	deposition	glaciation	abrasion
6.	shape of a glacial valley:	V-shaped	U-shaped	W-shaped

Name/Date _____

Earth Science 32

Unscramble each term

1. A deep crack in a glacier:

   sevacres _____

2. To crush: **mptcaco** _____

3. Loose rock fragments:

   ebrisd _____

4. Large loose rocks:

   oulbders _____

Name/Date _____

Earth Science 33

Circle T for true or F for false.
1. Floodplains are found on steep mountainsides. T F
2. A delta forms where a large river enters the ocean. T F
3. A river meander is an area with many rapids. T F
4. A canyon is a narrow valley with steep walls. T F
5. A river system includes the source, the tributaries, and the mouth. T F

Name/Date _____

Earth Science 34

Draw a line to match each clue to the best term.

1.	any precious stone	amethyst
2.	the hardest stone	emerald
3.	fossilized tree sap	gem
4.	a purple stone	amber
5.	a green gem	diamond

Name/Date _____

Earth Science 35

Circle the term that best fits each clue.
1. large dark green seaweed:
   kelp   plankton   diatom
2. under the ocean:
   coastal   undersea   hydrothermal
3. constructive:
   unchanging   breaking down   building up
4. destructive:
   unchanging   breaking down   building up

Science Vocabulary Warm-ups:
Atmospheric & Space Science

Name/Date _____

Atmospheric & Space Science 1

Circle T for true or F for false.
1. Air pressure is the weight of air pushing down. T F
2. Falling rain is an example of evaporation. T F
3. The earth's atmosphere is composed of gases. T F
4. The weather is the current condition of outdoor air. T F
5. A rainstorm is an example of climate. T F

Name/Date _____

Atmospheric & Space Science 2

Draw a line to match each instrument to what it measures.

1. anemometer   air pressure
2. barometer   temperature
3. hygrometer   precipitation
4. thermometer   humidity
5. rain gauge   wind speed

Name/Date _____

Atmospheric & Space Science 3

Circle the term that matches each clue.

1. long dry period: pollution   ozone   drought
2. greenhouse effect: global warming   global cooling pollution
3. a form of oxygen: nitrogen   drought   ozone
4. man-made impurities: pollution   nitrogen   drought
5. world-wide: local   coastal   global

Name/Date _____

Atmospheric & Space Science 4

Unscramble each term.
1. A small rocky body orbiting the sun: **teroidas** _____
2. An icy body with a long tail orbiting the sun: **otcme** _____
3. Rock or metal from space entering the earth's atmosphere: **eormet** _____
4. Part of a meteor that lands on earth: **etemoriet** _____

Name/Date _____

Atmospheric & Space Science 5

Fill in the missing letters.
1. A group of bright stars associated with a story: c __ __ st __ __ la __ i __ n
2. A large group of stars: g __ l __ __ y
3. A large sphere of burning gas in space: s __ __ __
4. A collapsed star with extremely powerful gravity: b __ __ __ k h __ __ e

Science Vocabulary Warm-ups:
Atmospheric & Space Science

Name/Date _____

Atmospheric & Space Science 6

Circle the term that best fits each clue.

1. Mars, Venus, Earth:
    outer planets   inner planets
2. revolve around another body:
    orbit   collapse
3. Neptune, Saturn, Jupiter:
    outer planets   inner planets
4. a large body circling a star:
    comet   planet

Name/Date _____

Atmospheric & Space Science 7

Fill in the missing letters.

The four (1) __ n __ er p __ __ n __ __ s
are also called the (2) r __ __ __ y, or

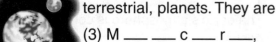

terrestrial, planets. They are
(3) M __ __ c __ r __,
(4) V __ __ __ __,
(5) E __ __ __ __ , and (6) M __ __ __.

Name/Date _____

Atmospheric & Space Science 8

Fill in the missing letters.

The four (1) __ u __ e __ planets are also
called the (2) g __ s __ o __ s planets. They
are (3) J __ p __ t __ r,

(4) S __ t __ r __,

(5) U __ __ n __ s, and

(6) N __ __ t __ __ e.

Name/Date _____

Atmospheric & Space Science 9

Draw a line to match each clue to the best term.

1. our galaxy   telescope
2. instrument to see
    distant objects   local group
3. grouped close
    together   nebula
4. galaxies close to
    the Milky Way   Milky Way
5. a cloud of stars, gas,
    and dust in space   cluster

Name/Date _____

Atmospheric & Space Science 10

Circle the best term for each definition.

1. a scientist who studies the universe:	cosmologist	geologist	biologist
2. to fall in:	expand	retreat	collapse
3. planets orbiting a star:	solar system	universe	local group
4. the universe:	Milky Way	everything in space	local group
5. the most common element in the universe:	oxygen	hydrogen	iron
6. a light gas that does not burn:	iron	nickel	helium

Science Vocabulary Warm-ups:
Atmospheric & Space Science

Name/Date _____

Atmospheric & Space Science 11

Fill in the missing letters.

1. The earth spins around its ax __ __.
2. G __ __ __ ity pulls things toward the earth's surface.
3. The r __ t __ t __ __ n of the earth causes day and night.
4. The earth's r __ __ __ l __ t __ __ n around the sun takes a year.

Name/Date _____

Atmospheric & Space Science 12

Write the letter of the best word on each line.

A. Hemisphere   B. equator   C. seasons   D. tilt

The (1) _____ of the earth's axis causes the (2) _____. When it is winter in the Northern (3) _____, it is summer in the Southern Hemisphere. The (4) _____ separates the Northern Hemisphere from the Southern Hemisphere.

Name/Date _____

Atmospheric & Space Science 13

Fill in the missing letters.

The Milky Way is a (1) b __ __ re __

(2) s __ __ r __ l galaxy. Many other galaxies are

(3) e __ __ __ pti __ __ __. Sometimes, galaxies

(4) c __ __ l __ d __, or run into each other.

Name/Date _____

Atmospheric & Space Science 14

Circle the term that best fits each clue.

1. a rotating neutron star: supernova   pulsar
2. a stage in the death of a medium-sized star:
             red giant   neutron star
3. the sudden brief explosion of a star: pulsar   supernova
4. a bright object at the edge of the universe:
             red giant   quasar

Name/Date _____

_____

Atmospheric & Space Science 15

Unscramble each boldface term.

1. Cooler dark spots on the surface of the sun are called **otnssups**.

   _____

2. A powerful explosion in the sun's atmosphere is a solar **elfar**.

   _____

3. During a total solar eclipse, the sun's **roacno**

   _____

   is visible.

4. When the moon comes between the sun and the earth, there is a solar **lipeesc**.

   _____

5. The invisible light waves responsible for sunburns are called **oleurtavilt**

   _____

   rays.

Science Vocabulary Warm-ups:
Atmospheric & Space Science

Name/Date _____

Atmospheric & Space Science 16

Place the letter of the term next to the correct definition.

A. astronomer   B. imaginary   C. Orion
D. constellation   E. Ursa Major

_____ 1. group of stars connected with a story

_____ 2. scientist who studies stars

_____ 3. mythic

_____ 4. constellation, the great bear

_____ 5. constellation, the hunter

Name/Date _____

Atmospheric & Space Science 17

Fill in the missing letters.

1. very small planets, including Pluto:
   d ___ a ___ f planets
2. an area at the edge of the solar system:
   K ___ ___ p ___ r b ___ ___ t
3. An area of space between Mars and Jupiter:
   a ___ ___ e ___ ___ id b ___ ___ t
4. a crater caused by a meteorite:
   ___ ___ ___ a ___ t crater
5. Objects in space: b ___ ___ ___ ___ s

Name/Date _____

Atmospheric & Space Science 18

Write the correct term from the box on each line.

warm front	transpiration
cold front	El Niño
evaporation	

1. a warm ocean current that creates unusual weather _____

2. a cool air mass moving in on a warm air mass _____

3. a warm air mass moving in on a cool air mass _____

4. water vapor moving into the air through the leaves of plants _____

5. to change from a liquid to a gas _____

Name/Date _____

Atmospheric & Space Science 19

Circle T for true or F for false.
1. A droplet is a very large water drop. T F
2. Fog consists of water droplets suspended in the air. T F
3. Smog is fog mixed with smoke or other pollutants. T F
4. A drizzle is a heavy downpour. T F
5. If the air is moist, it is extremely dry. T F

Name/Date _____

Atmospheric & Space Science 20

Unscramble the terms.
1. light waves invisible to humans, used in remote controls: **nfridare** _____
2. different forms of the same thing:
   rinsativao _____
3. an element present in living things:
   arbnco _____
4. to move around:
   ctelircua _____

Science Vocabulary Warm-ups: Atmospheric & Space Science

Name/Date _____

Atmospheric & Space Science 21

Circle the correct term to match the definition.
1. High clouds, often made of ice:
   cumulus   stratus   cirrus
2. Low, fluffy-looking clouds:
   cumulus   stratus   cirrus
3. An even blanket of low gray clouds:
   cumulus   stratus   cirrus
4. Mid-level clouds in bunches:
   altocumulus   cirrus   nimbus
5. Rainclouds: altocumulus   cirrus   nimbus

Name/Date _____

Atmospheric & Space Science 22

Unscramble each term.
1. Rain, hail, and snow: **pipitaorectin**

   _____

2. Repeating periods of heat and cold:
   weather **tprnate** _____

3. ice chunks: **ihla** _____

4. ice crystals: **nsow** _____

5. liquid water drops: **arin** _____

Name/Date _____

Atmospheric & Space Science 23

Circle T for true or F for false.

1. Humidity is a kind of mud caused by
   heavy runoff. T   F

2. In determining relative humidity,
   temperature is important. T   F

3. The dew point is a temperature. T   F

4. Precipitation is part
   of the water cycle. T   F

Name/Date _____

Atmospheric & Space Science 24

Place the letter of the correct word in each blank.
**A. lunar, B. eclipse, C. moon, D. phases,
E. quarter**

The (1) _____ rotates around the earth. The word
(2) _____ is an adjective that means "relating to
the moon." The moon's shapes, or (3) _____,
include full, half, and (4) _____. Sometimes, the
shadow of the earth causes a strange
phenomenon called an (5) _____.

Name/Date _____

Atmospheric & Space Science 25

Circle the best term for each description.

1. large tropical storm with high winds and heavy rain:	hurricane	tornado	front
2. a powerful funnel-shaped wind storm:	hurricane	tornado	front
3. rainstorm with thunder and lightning:	hurricane	thunderstorm	front
4. discharge of electricity from clouds:	front	magnetism	lightning
5. where two different air masses meet:	front	tornado	hurricane
6. a body of warm or cool air:	hurricane	tornado	air mass

Science Vocabulary Warm-ups: Physical Science

Name/Date _____

_____

Physical Science 1

Fill in the missing letters.

1. colors in white light:

   sp __ __ t __ __ m

2. wavelengths between light and radio waves:

   i __ __ __ ar __ d

3. invisible waves that cause sunburns:

   ul __ __ a __ __ ol __ t

4. colorful arc in sky created by refraction:

   r __ __ n __ __ w

5. the study of light:

   o __ __ i __ s

Name/Date _____

Physical Science 2

Circle the best term for each clue.
1. practical knowledge: fiber technology consumption
2. thread: metal gas fiber
3. iron: nonmetal metal fiber
4. carbon: nonmetal metal gas
5. precious metal: iron tin gold

Name/Date _____

Physical Science 3

Unscramble each term.
1. blocks all light (wood): **uepoqa** _____
2. can be seen through (glass): **antrarenspt**

   _____
3. light passes through (tracing paper): **tnanslrceut**

   _____
4. separates white light into a spectrum: **ipmrs** _____

Name/Date _____

Physical Science 4

Circle the best term for each clue.
1. a lens curved inward: concave convex hollow
2. a lens curved outward: concave convex hollow
3. ability to soak up: refraction reflection absorption
4. wave changes direction: refraction reflection absorption
5. wave bounces from a surface: refraction reflection absorption

Name/Date _____

Physical Science 5

Draw a line to match each clue to the correct term.
1. enlarge   telescope
2. instrument to see faraway things   lens
3. instrument to see very small things   binoculars
4. instrument with two enlarging lenses   microscope
5. glass curved to bend light   magnify

Science Vocabulary Warm-ups: Physical Science

Name/Date _____

Physical Science 6

Circle T for true or F for false.

1. The speed of sound is faster than the speed of light. T F
2. Vibration is fast side-to-side movement. T F
3. The loudness or softness of a musical note is its pitch. T F
4. A sonic boom happens when an airplane goes faster than the speed of sound. T F
5. When you travel at a subsonic speed, you are underwater. T F
6. When you travel at a supersonic speed, you are in a slow car. T F

Name/Date _____

Physical Science 7

Fill in the missing letters.

1. to swing back and forth rhythmically:
   o ___ ci ___ ___ a ___ ___
2. extreme point on a pendulum swing:
   a ___ ___ li ___ u ___ e
3. repeating: r ___ ___ e ___ ___ t ___ on
4. number of times something happens in a given amount of time:
   f ___ ___ ___ u ___ ___ c ___

Name/Date _____

Physical Science 8

Circle the best term for each example.

1. iron: metal   alloy   nonmetal
2. molten: metal   melted   feathery
3. quartz: metal   alloy   nonmetal
4. studies metals: geologist   metallurgist
5. brass: nonmetal   alloy   copper

Name/Date _____

Physical Science 9

Circle the numbers of the statements that are true.

1. H_2O is the chemical formula for water.
2. Flammability is an example of a chemical property.
3. An ice cube melting is a chemical change.
4. Water evaporating is a physical change.
5. Length is an example of a physical property.

Name/Date _____

Physical Science 10

Circle the best term to fit each example.

1. vinegar: acid   base   litmus
2. baking soda: acid   base   litmus
3. ammonia: acid   base   litmus
4. test paper: acid   base   litmus
5. lemon juice: acid   base   litmus

Science Vocabulary Warm-ups: Physical Science

Name/Date _____

Physical Science 11

Fill in the missing letters.

1. A c __ __ p __ n __ __ t is part of something.
2. A c __ mp __ __ n __ is a chemical combination of elements.
3. In a m __ __ t __ __ e, substances combine without a chemical reaction.
4. Salt dissolved in water is a s __ l __ t __ __ n.
5. Muddy water is a su __ __ p __ ns __ __ n.

Name/Date _____

Physical Science 12

Circle the best term for each description.

1. oxygen in the air: liquid   solid   gas
2. water at room temperature:
      liquid   solid   gas
3. ice: liquid   solid   gas
4. to change from solid to liquid:
      solidify   evaporate   melt
5. to change from liquid to solid:
      solidify   evaporate   melt

Name/Date _____

Physical Science 13

Fill in each blank with a term from the box.

1. An _____ has a nucleus and electrons.
2. A water _____ has two hydrogen atoms and one oxygen atom.
3. Hydrogen is an _____. All of its atoms are hydrogen atoms.
4. The _____ is a chart showing all of the elements.
5. Water has important physical and chemical _____.

element   atom   properties   molecule   periodic table

Name/Date _____

Physical Science 14

Use the clues to unscramble each term.

1. draw toward: **tatactr** _____
2. push away: **perel** _____
3. indicates magnetic north: **mpacsos**
   _____
4. plus: **opvesiti** _____
5. minus: **egiveatn** _____

Name/Date _____

Physical Science 15

Match the letter of each term to its definition.
A. neutron, B. proton, C. particle, D. nucleus, E. matter

____ 1.   a positively charged particle
____ 2.   a particle, neither positively nor negatively charged
____ 3.   the center of an atom
____ 4.   unit of matter (atom, molecule, proton)
____ 5.   substance

Science Vocabulary Warm-ups: Physical Science

Name/Date _____

Physical Science 16

Write the letter for the best word on each line.

A. current   B. conductor   C. amp   D. battery

1. An _____ is a basic unit of electricity.
2. A _____ changes chemical energy into electrical energy.
3. Copper is a good _____ of electricity.
4. Electrical _____ flows through the wires.

Name/Date _____

Physical Science 17

Unscramble each term.

1. route of electrical flow: **ircuict** _____
2. safety device to cut the flow of electricity:
   circuit **abrreke** _____
3. device that reduces or prevents flow of electricity:
   utlainsor _____

Name/Date _____

Physical Science 18

Fill in the missing letters.

1. speed up: a __ __ el __ r __ te
2. slow down: d __ c __ l __ r __ t __
3. speed in a certain direction: v __ l __ c __ t __
4. forward motion and resistance to slowing:
   m __ __ e __ t __ m

Name/Date _____

Physical Science 19

Unscramble each term

1. energy of a moving object: **etinikc** _____
2. unmoving: **ranaoytist** _____
3. changing energy from one form to another: **onvcoersin**
   _____
4. energy of an object at rest: **tienptaol** _____

Name/Date _____

_____

Physical Science 20

Write the best term from the box on each line.

coal	nonrenewable
energy	fossil fuels
petroleum	

We use (1) _____

to power our cars and generate

electricity. Most of the fuels

we use today were created

deep inside the earth. They are

called (2) _____.

Layers of (3) _____

formed from buried peat bogs.

Pools of (4) _____

formed from the remains of

tiny prehistoric sea creatures.

Once oil has been used, it

cannot be replaced, so it is a

(5) _____

resource.

Science Vocabulary Warm-ups: Physical Science

Name/Date _____

Physical Science 21

Fill in the missing letters.

1. Extra heat given off by machines as they work is w __ __ __ e heat.

2. Energy cannot be created or d __ __ tr __ y __ d.

3. H __ __ t is a form of energy.

4. H __ dr __ __ l __ __ tr __ __ __ ty is water power.

Name/Date _____

Physical Science 22

Circle the best definition for each term.

1. work: sweat   transfer energy

2. generate: create   use

3. renewable: irreplaceable   replaceable

4. additional: supplemental   mathematical

Name/Date _____

Physical Science 23

Fill in the missing letters to list alternative energy sources.

1. g __ __ th __ __ __ al

2. n __ __ l __ __ r

3. w __ __ __

4. so __ __ __

5. hy __ __ __ __ e __ __ __ t __ __ c

Name/Date _____

Physical Science 24

Match the letter of the term to the correct definition.

A. friction, B. inertia, C. energy, D. force, E. motion

____ 1. ability to do work

____ 2. stops or moves an object

____ 3. resistance between two moving objects

____ 4. movement

____ 5. resisting change

Name/Date _____

Physical Science 25

Read each term. Circle the best example.

1. simple machine   car   locomotive   wheel and axle

2. wedge   hook   ax   teeter-totter

3. lever   hook   ax   teeter-totter

4. inclined plane   ramp   wheel and axle   pulley

5. complex machine   ramp   scissors   wheel and axle

Science Vocabulary Warm-ups:
Science & Technology

Name/Date _____

Science & Technology 1

Write the best word or phrase from the box on each line.

1. Spinning rotor blades in a _____ change steam to electricity.
2. Oil _____ will not last forever.
3. Scientists are working to _____ the power of the wind.
4. On the great plains, farmers used _____ to pump water from wells.
5. A _____ near us uses several windmills to contribute clean energy to the grid.

Name/Date _____

Science & Technology 2

Circle the best word to match each clue.
1. air resistance: lift   airfoil   drag
2. pressure of air pushing a wing up:
   weight   lift   thrust
3. curved shape of the top of a wing:
   thrust   drag   airfoil
4. force experienced because of gravity:
   weight   thrust   lift
5. forward push: lift   thrust   airfoil

Name/Date _____

Science & Technology 3

Unscramble each term associated with nuclear reactions.
1. breaking apart the nucleus of an atom to release energy: **snsiofi** _____
2. giving off energetic particles: **rdioctaivea** _____
3. element used in some nuclear power plants: **aumnuri** _____
4. particle that strikes and breaks apart a nucleus in a chain reaction: **tonuenr** _____

Name/Date _____

Science & Technology 4

Fill in the missing letters.
1. A network for distributing power is a
   g __ __ d.
2. The electricity delivered to your house is
   a __ t __ __ n __ t __ __ g current.
3. Cables are part of the power
   d __ __ tr __ b __ t __ __ n system.
4. Before arriving at our home, electricity passed through a local
   s __ __ s __ __ t __ __ n.

Name/Date _____

Science & Technology 5

Write the letter of the correct word on each line.
   A. telegraph   B. transmit   C. Morse
   D. Marconi   E. device

Samuel (1) _____ developed a
code for the (2) _____, an electrical
(3) _____ designed to (4) _____
messages over a wire. Guglielmo
(5) _____ is famous for his work on the radio, a way
to send information through the air without a wire.

Science Vocabulary Warm-ups: Science & Technology

Name/Date _____

Science & Technology 6

Circle T for true or F for false.
1. Telecommunication is another word for a television news report. T F
2. An amplifier makes a signal more powerful. T F
3. An antenna can be used to send or receive radio signals. T F
4. A communications satellite is always located on top of a hill. T F
5. If a station transmits television signals, it is broadcasting. T F

Name/Date _____

Science & Technology 7

Fill in the missing letters.
1. Thomas Edison created the first practical ph __ __ __ g __ __ __ hic recordings.
2. A m __ g __ __ t __ c recording is stored on a special tape.
3. A d __ g __ t __ l recording is read by a laser.
4. The letters in the word l __ __ __ r stand for light amplification by stimulated emission of radiation.

Name/Date _____

Science & Technology 8

Circle the best term to fit each clue.

1. information sent:	signal	modem	decode
2. changes computer data to phone signals:	vacuum tubes	modem	circuit
3. a set of symbols used to talk to a computer:	chip	conductor	code
4. using integrated circuits or transistors:	insulated	electronic	portable
5. to change information into usable form:	decode	signal	fetch

---

Name/Date _____

Science & Technology 9

Unscramble each term.
1. A clock with a face and hands is an **laoang** _____ device.
2. A clock with numbers that change is a **giiatdl** _____ device.
3. A **itb** _____ can be either 0 or 1.
4. A **teyb** _____ is eight **sitb** _____.

Name/Date _____

Science & Technology 10

Fill in the missing letters to match each clue.
1. controls the flow of electricity in electronic devices: tra __ __ i __ t __ r
2. common element used in making semiconductors: s __ l __ c __ n
3. special chip that performs basic computer operations: m __ c __ opr __ c __ ss __ r
4. tiny silicon wafer with an integrated circuit: c __ __ p

Science Vocabulary Warm-ups: Science & Technology

Name/Date _____

Science & Technology 11

Circle T for true or F for false.
1. Printers, scanners, and cameras are peripherals. T F
2. A monitor is a kind of keyboard. T F
3. A page being printed from the computer is input. T F
4. A letter being typed into a word processing program is output. T F

Name/Date _____

Science & Technology 12

Unscramble each term.
1. data: **iatioronfmn** _____
2. a structured collection of information: **taasabde** _____
3. a system of linked computers: **nerktwo** _____
4. directions telling a computer how to perform a task: **rparogm** _____

Name/Date _____

Science & Technology 13

Fill in the missing letters.
1. the first workable model of a manufactured item:
   p __ __ t __ t __ __ e
2. eye scans and fingerprint keys are examples of:
   b __ __ m __ tr __ __ s
3. making machines very small:
   m __ ni __ t __ ri __ __ t __ __ n

Name/Date _____

Science & Technology 14

Circle the best term.
1. material composed of plant cell walls:
   synthetic   cellulose
2. to reuse: recycle   synthesize
3. crushed wood used in papermaking: polyester   pulp
4. a moving belt that transports materials: conveyor   turbine

Name/Date _____

_____

Science & Technology 15

Match each term to the best definition.

A. polyester
B. wool
C. plastic
D. rayon
E. synthetic

_____ 1. anything that is man-made or artificial

_____ 2. a moldable synthetic material

_____ 3. synthetic fabric made from plant material

_____ 4. a synthetic fabric made from chemicals

_____ 5. a natural fabric made from sheep hair

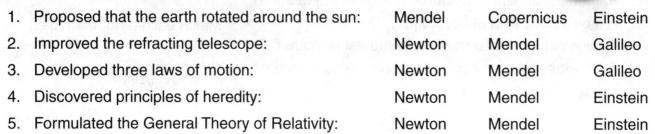

Science Vocabulary Warm-ups: Science & Technology

Name/Date _____

Science & Technology 16

Circle the scientist that fits each famous discovery.

1.	Proposed that the earth rotated around the sun:	Mendel	Copernicus	Einstein
2.	Improved the refracting telescope:	Newton	Mendel	Galileo
3.	Developed three laws of motion:	Newton	Mendel	Galileo
4.	Discovered principles of heredity:	Newton	Mendel	Einstein
5.	Formulated the General Theory of Relativity:	Newton	Mendel	Einstein

---

Name/Date _____

Science & Technology 17

Write the letter of the correct scientist on each line.
A. Pasteur   B. Curie
C. Pascal   D. Franklin   E. Faraday

_____ 1. founder of electrochemistry

_____ 2. demonstrated that microbes cause disease

_____ 3. discovered radioactivity

_____ 4. proposed that electricity flowed

_____ 5. studied fluid pressure and invented the barometer

Name/Date _____

Science & Technology 18

Unscramble each term.

1. Field biologists track wolves with radio **smrtarsteitn.** _____

2. The **lznidseatniaio** _____ process creates freshwater from salt water.

3. **tnevsanocori** _____ practices help preserve natural resources.

4. Something added to the environment that is harmful to living things is called **oplinoutl.** _____

Name/Date _____

Science & Technology 19

Circle T for true or F for false.

1. Compost is decayed plant matter. T F
2. Generating energy from ocean waves is called incineration. T F
3. Methane is an endangered rain forest plant. T F
4. A landfill is a waste management facility. T F
5. Junk yards recover scrap metals. T F

Name/Date _____

Science & Technology 20

Fill in the missing letters.

1. Using DNA information to change plants and animals is g __ n __ t __ c engineering.

2. P __ st __ c __ d __ s kill insects that destroy crops, but they can harm wildlife.

3. B __ __ l __ g __ c __ l pest control is a way to protect crops without insecticides.

Standards Correlation

From NCSESA, National Research Council, Grades 5–8

(Numbers refer to page numbers in *Jumpstarters for Science Vocabulary*.)

Science as Inquiry
Content standard A: Abilities necessary to do scientific inquiry: 2–8
Understandings about scientific inquiry: 2–8

Physical Science
Content standard B: Properties and changes of properties in matter: 5, 28, 32–36
Motions and forces: 32–36
Transfer of energy: 32–36

Life Science
Content Standard C: Structure and function in living systems: 9–19
Reproduction and heredity: 10, 11, 13, 18,
Regulation and behavior: 9–13, 19
Populations and ecosystems: 9, 11–13
Diversity and adaptations of organisms: 9–13, 19

Earth and Space Science
Content Standard D: Structure of the earth system: 20–26
Earth's history: 20–24, 26, 35
Earth in the solar system: 4, 25, 27–31

Science and Technology
Content Standard E: Abilities of technological design: 32, 35–40
Understandings about science and technology: 23, 30, 32, 35–40

Science in Personal and Social Perspectives
Content standard F: Personal health: 14–19
Populations, resources, and environments: 18, 23, 27, 29–31, 35–40
Natural hazards: 18, 20, 21, 27, 30, 31
Risks and benefits: 18, 20, 21, 36–40
Science and technology in society: 20, 23, 27, 30–32, 35–40

History and Nature of Science
Content Standard F: Science as a human endeavor: 1–3, 5, 7, 8, 23, 27, 29–32, 35–40
Nature of science: 2, 3, 5, 7
History of science: 30, 40

Answer Keys

General Science 1 (p. 2)
1. particle   2. method
3. science   4. expand
5. contract

General Science 2 (p. 2)
1. fact   2. system   3. cause
4. effect

General Science 3 (p. 2)
1. concept, idea
2. observe, watch
3. compare, find similarities
4. contrast, find differences
5. record, write down or save

General Science 4 (p. 2)
1. conclusion   2. data
3. collect   4. analysis   5. logic

General Science 5 (p. 2)
1. theory   2. hypothesis
3. experiment   4. identify
5. repeat

General Science 6 (p. 3)
1. word   2. mesh
3. basic   4. complicated
5. combination

General Science 7 (p. 3)
1. state, temporary form
2. force, energy
3. fundamental, basic
4. flow, move
5. unit, part

General Science 8 (p. 3)
1. investigate   2. technique
3. measure   4. condition
5. substance

General Science 9 (p. 3)
1. Finite   2. Infinite
3. Supplemental
4. phenomenon

General Science 10 (p. 3)
1. F 2. T 3. F 4. T 5. F

General Science 11 (p. 4)
1. density   2. speed
3. mass   4. volume
5. weight

General Science 12 (p. 4)
1. instrument   2. happen
3. plentiful   4. beginning
5. change

General Science 13 (p. 4)
1. True   2. False   3. True
4. False

General Science 14 (p. 4)
1. kilogram, a thousand grams
2. gram, basic metric unit of weight
3. milligram, a thousandth of a gram
4. millimeter, a thousandth of a meter
5. centimeter, a hundredth of a meter

General Science 15 (p. 4)
1. temperature   2. Celsius
3. degree   4. Fahrenheit

General Science 16 (p. 5)
1. absorb   2. balance
3. buoyancy   4. characteristic
5. classify

General Science 17 (p. 5)
1. width, diameter
2. most important, dominant
3. judge results, evaluate
4. data supporting a conclusion, evidence
5. diagram showing steps, flow chart

General Science 18 (p. 5)
1. function   2. inference
3. investigate   4. metric
5. model

General Science 19 (p. 5)
1. movement   2. thing
3. noticing   4. stage
5. foretell

General Science 20 (p. 5)
1. purpose   2. sequence
3. property
4. scientific explanations
5. scientific procedures

General Science 21 (p. 6)
1. Venn diagram   2. volume
3. thriving   4. variables
5. transfer

General Science 22 (p. 6)
1. stable   2. structure
3. technique   4. system

General Science 23 (p. 6)
1. sequence   2. result
3. precise   4. segment
5. name

General Science 24 (p. 6)
1. T 2. F 3. T 4. F 5. F

General Science 25 (p. 6)
1. constant   2. characteristic
3. decay   4. average

General Science 26 (p. 7)
1. equilibrium   2. imbalance

General Science 27 (p. 7)
1. reasonable   2. quantify
3. increase   4. response

General Science 28 (p. 7)
1. study   2. series
3. test   4. valid

General Science 29 (p. 7)
1. collide, run into each other
2. absolute, does not change
3. principles, fundamental rules or laws
4. relative, depends upon changing conditions

General Science 30 (p. 7)
1. scientific law
2. scientific model
3. scientific theory
4. scientific method
5. scientific evidence

General Science 31 (p. 8)
1. reliable, dependable
2. stationary, unmoving
3. variation, difference
4. transport, carry
5. synthesis, combining

General Science 32 (p. 8)
1. T 2. F 3. F 4. T

General Science 33 (p. 8)
1. regulate   2. random
3. reject   4. dehydrate
5. cyclic

General Science 34 (p. 8)
1. frequency
2. interrelationship
3. probable
4. recede
5. advance

General Science 35 (p. 8)
1. replicate, copy
2. submerge, sink
3. boundary, limit
4. inorganic, nonliving
5. significance, importance

Life Science 1 (p. 9)
1. ecology   2. community
3. biosphere 4. environment
5. adaptation

Life Science 2 (p. 9)
1. classification 2. nonliving
3. organisms   4. species

Life Science 3 (p. 9)
1. carnivores   2. herbivores
3. omnivores

Life Science 4 (p. 9)
1. T 2. F 3. T 4. T 5. F

Life Science 5 (p. 9)
1. mammal, has fur or hair
2. reptile, has scales
3. amphibian, lives part of life on land and part in water
4. bird, has feathers
5. mollusk, is an invertebrate

Life Science 6 (p. 10)
1. calf   2. eye color
3. diving 4. forest 5. kitten

Life Science 7 (p. 10)
1. C 2. A 3. D 4. B

Life Science 8 (p. 10)
1. membrane, a thin wall or layer
2. cytoplasm, contents of a cell, except the nucleus
3. cell, a basic unit of life
4. organelles, tiny structures with special tasks
5. nucleus, control center of a cell

Life Science 9 (p. 10)
1. F 2. T 3. T 4. F 5. F

Life Science 10 (p. 10)
1. camouflage   2. prey
3. mimicry   4. extinction
5. predator

Life Science 11 (p. 11)
1. branch, crown 3. cone
4. needle, limb

Life Science 12 (p. 11)
1. D 2. A 3. C 4. B 5. E

Life Science 13 (p. 11)
1. photosynthesis 2. leaf
3. oxygen   4. chlorophyll
5. carbon dioxide

Life Science 14 (p. 11)
1. T 2. F 3. T 4. T

Life Science 15 (p. 11)
1. ovary   2. stigma
3. pollen 4. petal 5. pistil

Life Science 16 (p. 12)
1. exchange   2. utility
3. biome   4. physical
5. distribution

Life Science 17 (p. 12)
1. population, group
2. source, origin
3. convert, change
4. structure, organization
5. materials, substances

Life Science 18 (p. 12)
1. respiration   2. digestion
3. excretion   4. circulation
5. multicellular

Life Science 19 (p. 12)
1. T 2. F 3. T 4. T

Life Science 20 (p. 12)
1. protozoa 2. defend 3. pest
4. descendant   5. survive

Life Science 21 (p. 13)
1. B 2. C 3. A 4. D

Life Science 22 (p. 13)
1. plasma   2. sponge
3. spore   4. crustacean
5. virus

Life Science 23 (p. 13)
1. beetle, kind of insect
2. protoplasm, living matter
3. mutualism, two species benefiting one another
4. live birth, not hatched from an egg
5. parasite, a species living at the expense of another

Life Science 24 (p. 13)
1. gills, respiratory organ of a fish
2. mates, goose and gander
3. internal, inside
4. external, outside
5. response, reaction

Life Science 25 (p. 13)
1. warm-blooded 2. arthropods
3. blue-green algae
4. competition   5. exoskeleton

Human Body 1 (p. 14)
1. calf   2. forearm
3. instep   4. thigh
5. abdomen

Human Body 2 (p. 14)
1. cycle   2. organ
3. tissue   4. organ system

Human Body 3 (p. 14)
1. central nervous system
2. brain   3. nerves
4. spinal cord 5. stimulus

Human Body 4 (p. 14)
1. C 2. B 3. A 4. E 5. D

Human Body 5 (p. 14)
1. vein   2. artery
3. capillary 4. artery, vein
5. pulmonary artery

Human Body 6 (p. 15)
1. digestive   2. stomach
3. intestines   4. esophagus
5. liver

Human Body 7 (p. 15)
1. coagulation   2. red
3. white   4. platelets
5. plasma

Human Body 8 (p. 15)
1. B 2. D/A 3. A/D 4. C

Human Body 9 (p. 15)
1. legs   2. hips   3. knee
4. chest 5. chest

Human Body 10 (p. 15)
1. D 2. B 3. E 4. C 5. A

Human Body 11 (p. 16)
1. nutrients   2. pyramid
3. minerals   4. calorie
5. Vitamin

Human Body 12 (p. 16)
1. optic   2. auditory
3. dentin 4. saliva 5. retina

Human Body 13 (p. 16)
1. gland   2. endocrine
3. adrenal   4. pancreas

Human Body 14 (p. 16)
1. excretory 2. kidney
3. bladder   4. skin
5. urethra

Human Body 15 (p. 16)
1. F 2. T 3. F 4. F 5. T

Human Body 16 (p. 17)
1. D 2. C 3. A 4. B

Human Body 17 (p. 17)
1. C 2. D 3. A 4. B

Human Body 18 (p. 17)
1. T 2. F 3. T 4. T 5. F

Human Body 19 (p. 17)
1. enamel   2. dentin
3. root   4. crown 5. gums

Human Body 20 (p. 17)
1. molars   2. incisors
3. deciduous 4. permanent
5. jaw

Human Body 21 (p. 18)
1. gene   2. chromosome
3. DNA   4. molecule
5. heredity

Human Body 22 (p. 18)
1. bacteria   2. inoculation
3. virus   4. pathogen

Human Body 23 (p. 18)
1. B 2. A 3. D 4. C

Human Body 24 (p. 18)
1. fitness   2. flexibility
3. aerobic   4. endurance

Human Body 25 (p. 18)
1. C 2. A 3. E 4. B 5. D

Human Body 26 (p. 19)
1. A 2. E 3. C 4. B 5. D

Human Body 27 (p. 19)
1. balance   2. inner ear
3. semicircular canals 4. sensor

Human Body 28 (p. 19)
1. retina 2. lens 3. iris
4. pupil 5. cornea

Human Body 29 (p. 19)
2. sweet 3. sour   4. salty
5. bitter
Listed foods will vary.

Human Body 30 (p. 19)
1. stimulus   2. pain
3. sensitive   4. irritation
5. dermis

Earth Science 1 (p. 20)
1. crust   2. inner core
3. mantle   4. outer core

Earth Science 2 (p. 20)
1. tectonics   2. continent
3. continental drift 4. plate

Earth Science 3 (p. 20)
1. fault   2. earthquake
3. wave   4. seismograph

Earth Science 4 (p. 20)
1. seismology, study of
   earthquakes
2. shallow, near the surface
3. tsunami, ocean wave caused
   by an earthquake
4. tremor, shaking
5. magnitude, size

Earth Science 5 (p. 20)
1. seismometer   2. interior
3. exterior   4. epicenter
5. occur

Earth Science 6 (p. 21)
1. volcanic   2. ash
3. basalt   4. pumice
5. obsidian

Earth Science 7 (p. 21)
1. C 2. D 3. B 4. E 5. A

Earth Science 8 (p. 21)
1. toxic   2. explosive
3. solidify   4. eruption

Earth Science 9 (p. 21)
1. E 2. C 3. D 4. B 5. A

Earth Science 10 (p. 21)
1. rock cycle 2. sedimentary
3. igneous   4. pressure
5. metamorphic

Earth Science 11 (p. 22)
1. marble 2. slate   3. granite
4. crystal 5. transform

Earth Science 12 (p. 22)
1. sandstone, sand
2. conglomerate; pebbles, sand,
   and clay
3. shale, clay
4. limestone, dissolved shells

Earth Science 13 (p. 22)
1. strata   2. erosion
3. weathering 4. conservation
5. resistant

Earth Science 14 (p. 22)
1. luster 2. hardness
3. color   4. streak color
5. crystal shape

Earth Science 15 (p. 22)
1. quartz 2. mineral 3. copper
4. pyrite 5. sulfur

Earth Science 16 (p. 23)
1. renewable resource, forests
2. nonrenewable resource, oil
3. alternative energy source,
   wind energy
4. pollution, smog

Earth Science 17 (p. 23)
1. anthracite 2. bituminous
3. fossils

Earth Science 18 (p. 23)
1. C 2. D 3. B 4. A

Earth Science 19 (p. 23)
1. uplifted   2. exposed
3. deposited 4. compressed

Earth Science 20 (p. 23)
1. fossilization   2. hardened
3. skeletons 4. Impressions
5. shells

Earth Science 21 (p. 24)
1. A 2. C 3. B 4. D

Earth Science 22 (p. 24)
1. iceberg   2. retreating
3. advancing 4. valley
5. ice sheet

Earth Science 23 (p. 24)
1. stalactites 2. stalagmite
3. cavern   4. corrosive
5. dissolve

Earth Science 24 (p. 24)
1. coastal   2. arch
3. stack   4. undercutting

Earth Science 25 (p. 24)
1. D 2. A 3. E 4. B 5. C

Earth Science 26 (p. 25)
1. E 2. C 3. B 4. D 5. A

Earth Science 27 (p. 25)
1. current 2. depth
3. salinity 4. marine

Earth Science 28 (p. 25)
1. trenches 2. shallow
3. surface 4. island
5. hot spot

Earth Science 29 (p. 25)
1. mid-ocean 2. zone
3. sonar 4. sea floor
5. continent

Earth Science 30 (p. 25)
1. Tides 2. gravity 3. bulge
4. spring 5. neap

Earth Science 31 (p. 26)
1. glacier 2. moraine
3. ice age 4. abrasion
5. deposition 6. U-shaped

Earth Science 32 (p. 26)
1. crevasse 2. compact
3. debris 4. boulders

Earth Science 33 (p. 26)
1. F 2. T 3. F 4. T 5. T

Earth Science 34 (p. 26)
1. any precious stone, gem
2. the hardest stone, diamond
3. fossilized tree sap, amber
4. a purple stone, amethyst
5. a green gem, emerald

Earth Science 35 (p. 26)
1. kelp 2. undersea
3. building up 4. breaking down

Atmos. & Space Science 1 (p. 27)
1. T 2. F 3. T 4. T 5. F

Atmos. & Space Science 2 (p. 27)
1. anemometer, wind speed
2. barometer, air pressure
3. hygrometer, humidity
4. thermometer, temperature
5. rain gauge, precipitation

Atmos. & Space Science 3 (p. 27)
1. drought 2. global warming
3. ozone 4. pollution
5. global

Atmos. & Space Science 4 (p. 27)
1. asteroid 2. comet
3. meteor 4. meteorite

Atmos. & Space Science 5 (p. 27)
1. constellation 2. galaxy
3. star 4. black hole

Atmos. & Space Science 6 (p. 28)
1. inner planets 2. orbit
3. outer planets 4. planet

Atmos. & Space Science 7 (p. 28)
1. inner planets 2. rocky
3. Mercury 4. Venus
5. Earth 6. Mars

Atmos. & Space Science 8 (p. 28)
1. outer 2. gaseous
3. Jupiter 4. Saturn
5. Uranus 6. Neptune

Atmos. & Space Science 9 (p. 28)
1. Milky Way 2. telescope
3. cluster 4. local group
5. nebula

Atmos. & Space Science 10 (p. 28)
1. cosmologist 2. collapse
3. solar system
4. everything in space
5. hydrogen 6. helium

Atmos. & Space Science 11 (p. 29)
1. axis 2. gravity
3. rotation 4. revolution

Atmos. & Space Science 12 (p. 29)
1. D 2. C 3. A 4. B

Atmos. & Space Science 13 (p. 29)
1. barred 2. spiral
3. elliptical 4. collide

Atmos. & Space Science 14 (p. 29)
1. pulsar 2. red giant
3. supernova 4. quasar

Atmos. & Space Science 15 (p. 29)
1. sunspots 2. flare
3. corona 4. eclipse
5. ultraviolet

Atmos. & Space Science 16 (p. 30)
1. D 2. A 3. B 4. E 5. C

Atmos. & Space Science 17 (p. 30)
1. dwarf 2. Kuiper belt
3. asteroid belt 4. impact
5. bodies

Atmos. & Space Science 18 (p. 30)
1. El Niño 2. cold front
3. warm front 4. transpiration
5. evaporation

Atmos. & Space Science 19 (p. 30)
1. F 2. T 3. T 4. F 5. F

Atmos. & Space Science 20 (p. 30)
1. infrared 2. variations
3. carbon 4. circulate

Atmos. & Space Science 21 (p. 31)
1. cirrus 2. cumulus
3. stratus 4. altocumulus
5. nimbus

Atmos. & Space Science 22 (p. 31)
1. precipitation 2. pattern
3. hail 4. snow 5. rain

Atmos. & Space Science 23 (p. 31)
1. F 2. T 3. T 4. T

Atmos. & Space Science 24 (p. 31)
1. C 2. A 3. D 4. E 5. B

Atmos. & Space Science 25 (p. 31)
1. hurricane 2. tornado
3. thunderstorm 4. lightning
5. front 6. air mass

Physical Science 1 (p. 32)
1. spectrum 2. infrared
3. ultraviolet 4. rainbow
5. optics

Physical Science 2 (p. 32)
1. technology 2. fiber
3. metal 4. nonmetal
5. gold

Physical Science 3 (p. 32)
1. opaque 2. transparent
3. translucent 4. prism

Physical Science 4 (p. 32)
1. concave 2. convex
3. absorption 4. refraction
5. reflection

Physical Science 5 (p. 32)
1. enlarge, magnify
2. instrument to see faraway things, telescope
3. instrument to see very small things, microscope
4. instrument with two enlarging lenses, binoculars
5. glass curved to bend light, lens

45

Physical Science 6 (p. 33)
1. F 2. T 3. F 4. T 5. F
6. F

Physical Science 7 (p. 33)
1. oscillate   2. amplitude
3. repetition   4. frequency

Physical Science 8 (p. 33)
1. metal   2. melted
3. nonmetal   4. metallurgist
5. alloy

Physical Science 9 (p. 33)
1., 2., 4., and 5. should be circled.

Physical Science 10 (p. 33)
1. acid   2. base   3. base
4. litmus 5. acid

Physical Science 11 (p. 34)
1. component   2. compound
3. mixture   4. solution
5. suspension

Physical Science 12 (p. 34)
1. gas   2. liquid 3. solid
4. melt   5. solidify

Physical Science 13 (p. 34)
1. atom   2. molecule
3. element   4. periodic table
5. properties

Physical Science 14 (p. 34)
1. attract   2. repel
3. compass   4. positive
5. negative

Physical Science 15 (p. 34)
1. B 2. A 3. D 4. C 5. E

Physical Science 16 (p. 35)
1. C 2. D 3. B 4. A

Physical Science 17 (p. 35)
1. circuit   2. breaker
3. insulator

Physical Science 18 (p. 35)
1. accelerate 2. decelerate
3. velocity   4. momentum

Physical Science 19 (p. 35)
1. kinetic   2. stationary
3. conversion 4. potential

Physical Science 20 (p. 35)
1. energy   2. fossil fuels
3. coal   4. petroleum
5. nonrenewable

Physical Science 21 (p. 36)
1. waste   2. destroyed
3. Heat   4. Hydroelectricity

Physical Science 22 (p. 36)
1. transfer energy 2. create
3. replaceable 4. supplemental

Physical Science 23 (p. 36)
1. geothermal   2. nuclear
3. wind (or wave) 4. solar
5. hydroelectric

Physical Science 24 (p. 36)
1. C 2. D 3. A 4. E 5. B

Physical Science 25 (p. 36)
1. wheel and axle 2. ax
3. teeter-totter 4. ramp
5. scissors

Science & Technology 1 (p. 37)
1. turbine   2. reserves
3. harness   4. windmills
5. wind farm

Science & Technology 2 (p. 37)
1. drag   2. lift   3. airfoil
4. weight 5. thrust

Science & Technology 3 (p. 37)
1. fission   2. radioactive
3. uranium   4. neutron

Science & Technology 4 (p. 37)
1. grid   2. alternating
3. distribution 5. substation

Science & Technology 5 (p. 37)
1. C 2. A 3. E 4. B 5. D

Science & Technology 6 (p. 38)
1. F 2. T 3. T 4. F 5. T

Science & Technology 7 (p. 38)
1. phonographic 2. magnetic
3. digital   4. laser

Science & Technology 8 (p. 38)
1. signal   2. modem
3. code   4. electronic
5. decode

Science & Technology 9 (p. 38)
1. analog   2. digital
3. bit   4. byte, bits

Science & Technology 10 (p. 38)
1. transistor   2. silicon
3. microprocessor 4. chip

Science & Technology 11 (p. 39)
1. T 2. F 3. F 4. F

Science & Technology 12 (p. 39)
1. information 2. database
3. network   4. program

Science & Technology 13 (p. 39)
1. prototype   2. biometrics
3. miniaturization

Science & Technology 14 (p. 39)
1. cellulose   2. recycle
3. pulp   4. conveyor

Science & Technology 15 (p. 39)
1. E 2. C 3. D 4. A 5. B

Science & Technology 16 (p. 40)
1. Copernicus   2. Galileo
3. Newton   4. Mendel
5. Einstein

Science & Technology 17 (p. 40)
1. E 2. A 3. B 4. D 5. C

Science & Technology 18 (p. 40)
1. transmitters
2. desalinization
3. conservation
4. pollution

Science & Technology 19 (p. 40)
1. T 2. F 3. F 4. T 5. T

Science & Technology 20 (p. 40)
1. genetic   2. Pesticides
3. Biological